ELMER'S
Baby Record Book

Stick baby's photograph here

All about . . . .

Born on. . . . .

At . . . .

My Excited New Family

**My mummy and daddy were so thrilled when they found out
I was coming along!**

Mummy's name . . . .

Daddy's name . . . .

Stick scan photograph here

They thought I might be

☐ a boy

☐ a girl

My scan photograph was taken on . . . .

I was due to arrive on

. . . .

My family's favourite names were

. . . .

. . . .

The thought of having a baby made them feel

. . . .

Hello, World!

At last I arrived!

I was born on . . . .

in . . . . The time was . . . .

The weather was. . . . .

I was called . . . .

because . . . .

The story of how I arrived . . . .

. . . .

. . . .

. . . .

I weighed . . . .

I measured

. . . .

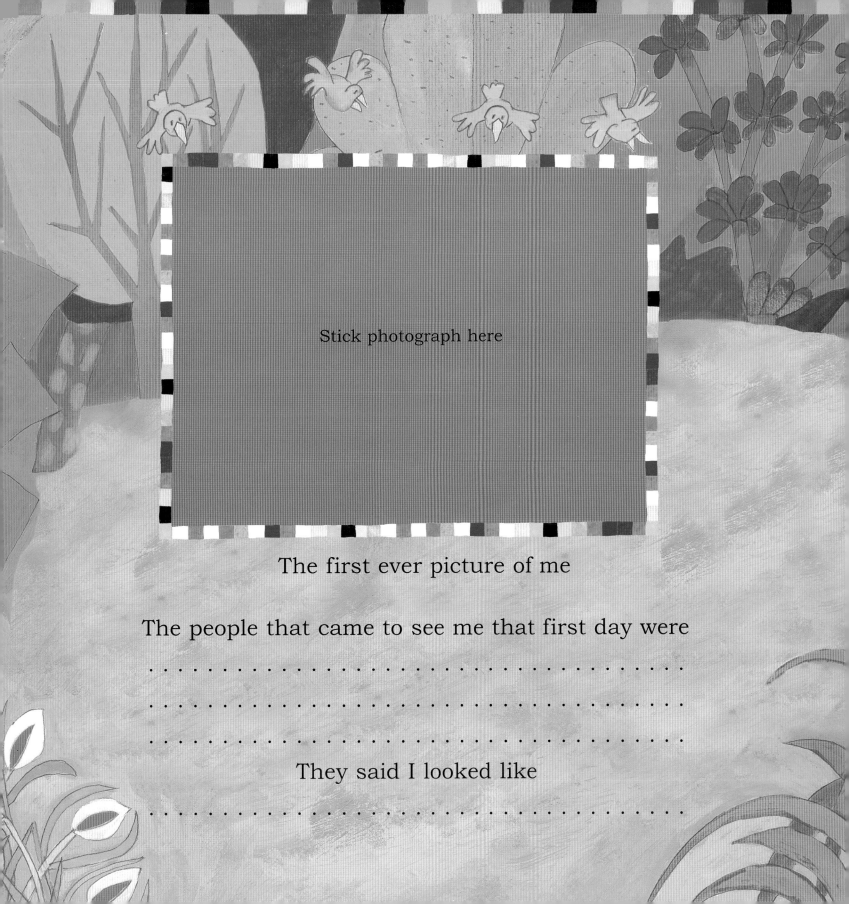

Stick photograph here

The first ever picture of me

The people that came to see me that first day were

. . . .

. . . .

. . . .

They said I looked like

. . . .

Special from Top to Toe!

It's funny to remember how tiny I used to be!

My eyes were . . . .   My hair was . . . .

Some special things about me. . . . .

. . . .

. . . .

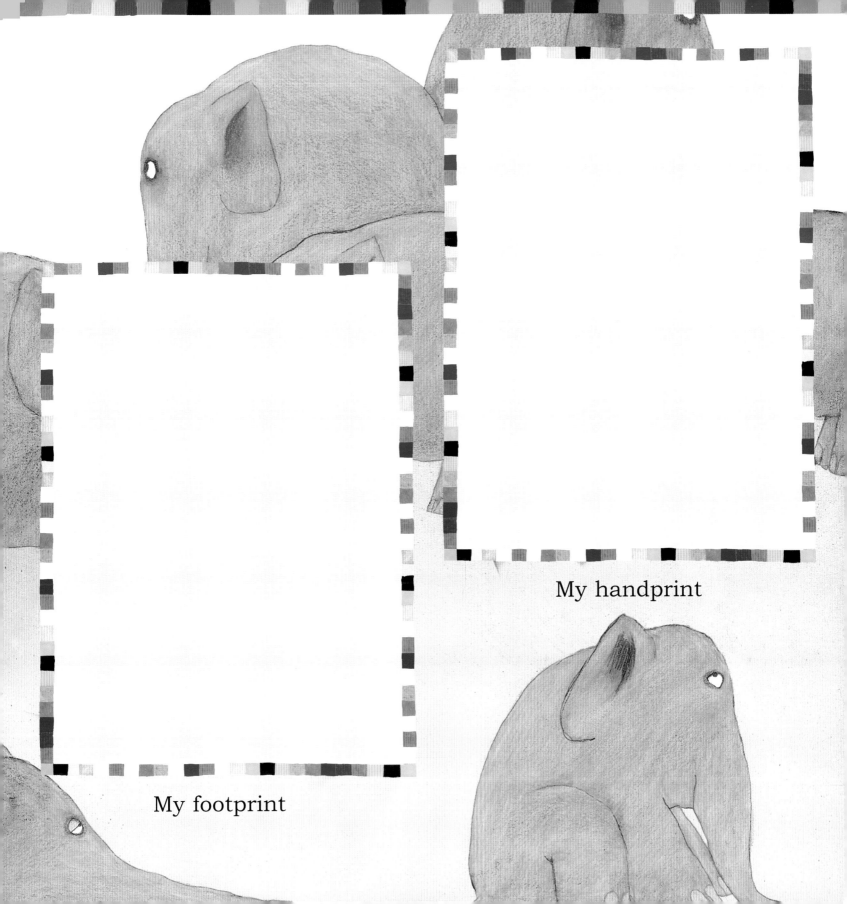

My handprint

My footprint

Coming Home

It was a very special day when I was wrapped up and taken home for the very first time.

Stick photograph here

I came home on . . . .

My first address was

. . . .

. . . .

Some of my first visitors were

. . . .

. . . .

My First Days

My family told everyone about me!

I used to like feeding best at . . . .

My sleepiest times were . . . .

Some of my cutest outfits were . . . .

. . . .

The little things that made me feel happy were . . . .

. . . .

. . . .

. . . .

My Family Tree

It makes me smile to think of all the different people that make up my family.

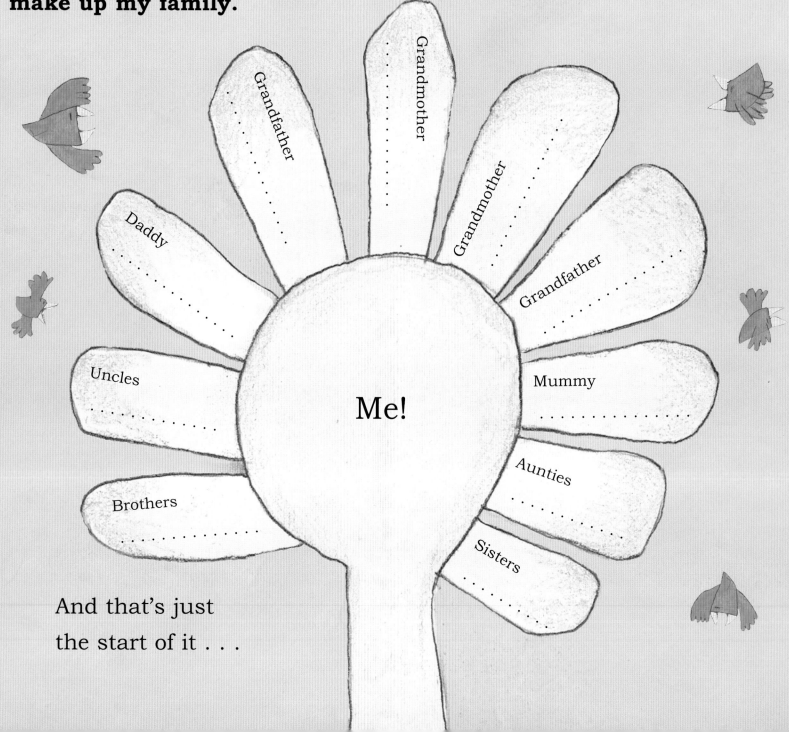

Grandfather

Grandmother

Grandmother

Daddy

Grandfather

Uncles

Me!

Mummy

Brothers

Aunties

Sisters

And that's just the start of it . . .

My Growth Chart

Every day I got that little bit longer, rounder and stronger.

Age	Height	Weight
. . . . .	. . . .	. . . . .
. . . . .	. . . .	. . . . .
. . . . .	. . . .	. . . . .
. . . . .	. . . .	. . . . .
. . . . .	. . . .	. . . . .
. . . . .	. . . .	. . . . .
. . . . .	. . . .	. . . . .
. . . . .	. . . .	. . . . .
. . . . .	. . . .	. . . . .
. . . . .	. . . .	. . . . .
. . . . .	. . . .	. . . . .

Important First Times

There were so many new things for me to learn and do!

First smile. . . . .

Held head up. . . . .

First immunisations . . . .

Rolled over . . . .

And rolled back again . . . .

Held a toy . . . .

Played with feet . . . .

First chuckle . . . .

Sat upright by myself

. . . .

First slept through the night

. . . .

Ate solid food . . . .

Clapped . . . .

First made kisses and waves

First steps

. . . .

. . . .

Crawled

First proper walk outside

. . . .

. . . .

Pulled myself to standing

First haircut. . . . .

. . . .

First words . . . .

Stood up . . . .

Went swimming . . . .

Getting Around

I found all sorts of funny ways to move around and reach my toys.

From stretching . . .

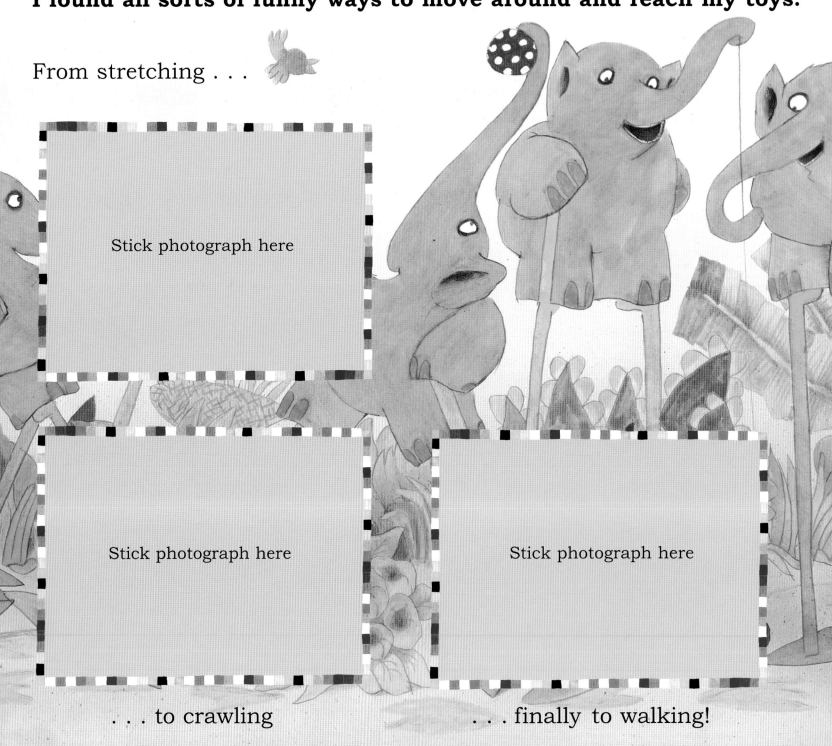

Stick photograph here

Stick photograph here

Stick photograph here

. . . to crawling

. . . finally to walking!

Mealtimes

**I started off with milk, then tried out
all kinds of delicious new things.**

My first taste of
solid food was. . . . .

I first drank from a cup when. . . . . . .

I first used my fingers . . . .

My favourite foods were

. . . .

. . . .

. . . .

. . . .

I wasn't so keen on

. . . .

. . . .

. . . .

. . . .

. . . .

Bathtimes

Bathtimes weren't just for washing – we had lots of fun and games!

My first bath was . . . .

I thought it was . . . .

My favourite bath toys were . . . . . .

. . . .

My first time in the big bath was

. . . .

Stick photograph here

Bedtimes

I slept a lot at first, in all kinds of sleepy positions!

I first slept in . . . . I moved to a cot when I was . . .

My favourite bedtime songs and stories were

. . . .

The things I liked to sleep with were

. . . .

Celebrations!

**There were lots of things
to celebrate during the
year that I arrived.**

There were parties for. . . . .

I was dressed up in . . . .

My Christening or Naming Day Celebration was. . . . .

Some of the special people that came were . . . .

. . . .

. . . .

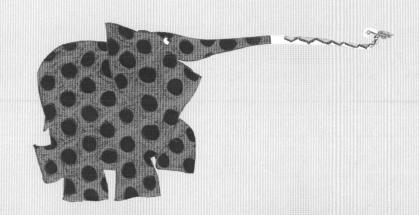

I enjoyed my first Christmas with

. . . .

Some of the best presents I received were

. . . .

. . . .

The happiest moments during Christmas Day were

. . . .

. . . .

Special Playmates

It didn't take long for me to meet all kinds of special new friends.

My first playmates were

. . . .

. . . .

. . . .

How we met

. . . .

. . . .

Stick photograph here

Me with

. . . .

Fun and Games

I invented lots of fun new ways to play!

My favourite games were

. . . .

. . . .

My favourite toys were

. . . .

. . . .

The things that made me chuckle were

. . . .

. . . .

The books I loved best were

. . . .

. . . .

Holidays

**There was lots to pack
for my first holiday!**

My first trip away was to

. . . .

I went with

. . . .

. . . .

The best things we did were

. . . .

. . . .

Stick photograph here

My funniest holiday snap

My First Birthday

At last I was ONE!

My first ever birthday was on

. . . .

We celebrated by . . . .

. . . .

I wore . . . .

My birthday cake was

. . . .

My guests were

. . . .

. . . .

. . . .

. . . .

. . . .

. . . .

. . . .

Special Memories

**There were lots of unforgettable times
during my first months.**

Special things to always remember . . . .

. . . .

Some of the funny things that made me unique . . . .

. . . .

. . . .

My family's favourite memory of me

. . . .

. . . .

. . . .

Stick photograph here

Hopes and Dreams . . . .

. . . .

. . . .

Plans for the Future . . . .

. . . .

. . . .

Me at . . . months